What Your Employees
Really Want From You

What Your Employees Really Want From You

✦

How to Dramatically Reduce Your Turnover by Cultivating Your Greatest Asset—Your Employees

Mark Byrne
With Craig A. Repp

iUniverse, Inc.
New York Lincoln Shanghai

What Your Employees Really Want From You
How to Dramatically Reduce Your Turnover by Cultivating Your Greatest Asset—Your Employees

iUniverse books may be ordered through booksellers or by contacting:

iUniverse
2021 Pine Lake Road, Suite 100
Lincoln, NE 68512
www.iuniverse.com
1-800-Authors (1-800-288-4677)

The views expressed in this work are solely those of the author and do not necessarily reflect the views of the publisher, and the publisher hereby disclaims any responsibility for them.
Cover design by Tammy Waldeck
Cover photograph by Tamsen Arabi

ISBN: 978-0-595-42045-2 (pbk)
ISBN: 978-0-595-86390-7 (ebk)

Printed in the United States of America

Successful people are always looking for opportunities to help others. Unsuccessful people are always asking, "What's in it for me?"

—Brian Tracy

I'd like to dedicate this book to several people:

To my wife, Dawn, whose never-ending belief in me has given me the courage and confidence to complete this mission. To her I am eternally grateful.

To every person I've ever had the privilege of working with over the past twenty-five years. Without all of you, this book would not have been possible.

To God.
Without Him, no great things would be possible.

Thank you all.

Mark Byrne

Contents

Preface

As you picked up this book, you may have been wondering, "How can I concern myself with what my employees want? I have a business to run. Why can't they just do their jobs?" At the same time, you are probably the sort of person who *does* want to know what they want. You like the idea of providing people with fulfilling work and the ability to earn good a living to raise their families.

Business executives often find themselves living two lives. In one, they are driven to maximize results in the workplace. Their careers rise and fall with the bottom line. This doesn't lend itself to a personal approach to business—to actually wondering what the employees *want*.

Their "second lives" outside their places of business are much more personal. They strive to be good family people and neighbors. They contribute their time and energy to their communities.

How can today's executive find an approach to business that's more congruent with their approach to life?

This book encourages you to strive for integration in your life—to bring your two worlds together. Mark Byrne challenges presidents, CEOs, and other executives to consider how their businesses could be healthier and more successful if they treated employees like neighbors and friends. You might say he's advocating the Golden Rule for businesspeople. Mark encourages you to treat your employees in ways that will foster loyalty, creativity, and enthusiasm, and he demonstrates how this can improve the work environment. Moreover, he makes a convincing case that this will improve your bottom line.

Mark is just the right person to publish such a book. I've worked with him in and out of the workplace, and I've seen how he treats people in every area of his life. He is an example of the congruence that he presents in this work. It shows in his life with his family, friends, and business associates. It also shows in his growing group of loyal customers. People like to be treated well, and Mark treats people well. Because of this, he is the perfect person to consult when you are considering how treating your employees affects you and your business.

Would you like your business to be more successful and more profitable? Would you like your place of business to be one of fulfillment and creativity for everyone involved? You can have both. Read on.

Craig A. Repp

Employees for Life

Having spent over twenty-five years in the American workplace, I've learned many things about the business world. Two very important lessons seem to stand above the rest:

1. **Hard work and persistence always pay off.**

2. **Take great care of your customers and they will take great care of you.**

I've worked for over a dozen different companies ranging from the "mom and pop" business with five employees all the way to a Fortune 500 worldwide corporation. All of my employers seemed to share my same two philosophies about persistence and the customer, but sadly most of them were severely lacking in the area of employee motivation.

With a few exceptions, these companies mostly saw employees as overhead or a necessary evil. Their HR departments existed primarily to avoid litigation from disgruntled employees and to meet legal requirements.

We all know what the initials HR stand for, but where has the *human* side of corporate America been hiding!?

During the past decade, I've been fortunate enough to have a great career as a successful salesperson. I attribute my success and good fortune to those two lessons I learned long ago.

My second lesson learned, "Take great care of your customers," has been one of the cornerstones to my success. To me, that statement means that if you take excellent care of your customers by providing superior service, they will take great care of you by giving you repeat business and great referrals. And if you're consistent with your actions year after year, you just might end up with a customer for life.

I reaped the rewards of success by following this philosophy and have gained many lifetime customers. I have always taken great care of my clients, and this approach has definitely made my career a successful one.

I have consistently treated my clients with respect, integrity, and honesty. I over-delivered as often as I could. I knew that if I wasn't taking great care of them, one of my competitors would.

Many CEOs, presidents, and executives have realized the same thing and have done phenomenal jobs caring for their customers. I once read that approximately 80 percent of all business owners, CEOs, and presidents of companies were at one time salespeople. They must have realized early in their sales careers exactly how important long-term clients could be for their success.

But somewhere in the midst of venturing out on their own or climbing the corporate ladder, many of these executives forget one of the keys to long-term success in business:

Take great care of your employees, just as you would your customers.

An employee is just as important to a business as the customer, if not more so. It's the employees that work behind the scenes to enable excellent customer care. In fact, your employees are the faces, voices, hands, and ears of your company to your customers. You can reap the reward of *customers for life* if your customers get the message that your company is committed to them. That message is going to be a lot clearer coming from a happy employee.

Why not take the same approach with your employees as you do with your customers? You could easily apply some of the great customer-care strategies that you've been using on your clients to get *employees for life*.

Let's face it: most children never say they want to be a grocery store clerk, loan processor, mechanic, salesperson, or human resources manager *when they grow up*. They all had dreams at one time of being something huge or glamorous, like an astronaut, movie star, firefighter, police officer, athlete, author, musician, or even president of the United States.

I'm not discouraging anyone out there still trying to achieve one of those dreams; in fact, quite the opposite. I admire such ambition immensely. But the reality is there are a finite number of those opportunities and at some point most of us have to choose (for whatever reasons) to do something else for a living.

But just because we aren't world-famous actors or politicians, that doesn't mean we can't enjoy what we do for a living! With the proper approach by you, the leader of your company, everyone can be enthusiastic about even the most mundane jobs.

The ideas presented in this book are about creating an environment that encourages employees to *want* to give more than just the bare minimum. They're about encouraging employees to *want* to come in earlier and stay later than they have to, because they know that the company (you) genuinely cares about their best interest and doesn't just see them as "overhead." If you follow these strategies, your employees will actually enjoy their (perhaps boring) jobs, secure in the knowledge that they are being as well cared for as your customers!

This book illustrates how a company should be run from an employee-centric perspective. By concentrating more on your employees, you *will* see a dramatic change in your turnover rates and your bottom line!

One last thing before we get started. I want to be very clear on my stance on employees. I believe they should be well taken care of but not spoiled. This book is a guideline for taking great care of all of your employees, but that does not mean tolerating the bad apples. Much like raising children, there's a big difference between raising a kid with love and discipline and simply spoiling him, giving him whatever he wants. *Huge difference.*

Having said that, let's move forward and have some fun!

The True Cost of Employee Turnover

Every company that hires employees will almost certainly lose some from time to time. Even though turnover is a part of running a successful business, how *many* you lose is really in your hands.

It has been estimated that it costs a company 150 percent of an employee's annual salary to replace that individual. For example, a $50,000 per year salaried employee will cost you up to $75,000 to replace.[1] Recruitment costs, training costs, and lost productivity and sales all add up quickly.

Knowing that turnover is this costly, why not invest the time, energy, and a little extra money to keep as many quality employees as possible?

While it is true that some employees will never work out no matter how well you treat them, they aren't our target audience. We want to focus on the remaining 70 to 80 percent of employees that are really worth keeping.

Have you calculated what your company's turnover rate is? Even an average turnover rate of 15 to 20 percent (U.S. national median average: 15.6 percent) for a small to medium company (forty employees) can cost a company in the neighborhood of $500,000–$600,000 annually in lost revenue (*profits*).

Let's look at this scenario. Let's say you did focus on reducing your turnover by implementing some of the ideas in this book, and, with all of your efforts, you cut your turnover rate by 50 percent, reducing your annual loss of employees to only four instead of eight. You will have saved your company between $250,000 and $300,000! I'm willing to bet that those funds could be reallocated pretty quickly towards new equipment, inventory, or even profit sharing.

Not only is losing an employee a financial burden on your company, but there's also the silent burden that almost always accompanies any employee exit: lost morale among your remaining employees.

Maybe you see the morale drop, maybe you don't, but I guarantee you that some people are going to miss that person when he or she is gone. What's that doing to your bottom line?

The following chapters were written to

- Give you new ideas to help your organization connect more with your employees, thus reducing your turnover rate.

- Give you some insight from the employees' perspective on how they like to be treated and what makes them work harder.

- Inspire you, the president/owner/CEO, to bring more to your organization, helping to make it one of the greatest companies in the world to work for!

Building a Sense of Ownership

It's very easy to figure out why executives put in the extra hours at the office. They're the ones responsible for the success of the company. If the business fails, it's their behind that's on the line, and they'll be the ones who will lose all of their hard work and, in the case of an owner, maybe even more (home, car, etc.).

The average employee doesn't own any portion of the company for which they work. So, should the company fail, the most she would be losing is her job. All she would need to do to regain what was lost is to go find another job.

Is it worthwhile to instill a sense of ownership in your employees? Absolutely! But you must find a way for them to genuinely care about their position in a similar fashion as you do, as owner or president.

There are several ways to accomplish this. If yours is a publicly held company, the most obvious way is to make your employees owners too, literally. Make it easy for them to buy a piece of the company in the form of shares of stock. They may not own as much of the company as you do, but they will have a vested interest in its overall success. This can be very motivating.

If yours is a privately held company, this can be a little bit more challenging, yet it is still attainable. Profit sharing is a similar approach to owning shares of stock, but in that case I would encourage you to provide monthly (or at least quarterly) reports to all the employees in your company so they are constantly reminded of what's ahead for everyone if they all work consistently hard. Sometimes a goal that's nine or ten months away is forgotten quickly.

How committed do you feel when your voice is heard and your ideas are executed? As an employee, some of the times that I felt most important were when I had the opportunity to assist in the decision-making process. When my opinion mattered, I felt responsible for the outcome of that decision. In a sense, my behind was on the line.

Employees realize that not all of their suggestions or input will be implemented, but when they feel like their words and experience can make a difference, they feel important.

*When people feel important, they will always
work harder than the ones who don't.*

If one of your departments is struggling to meet its goals, call a meeting (or several) and get the staff involved. Ask for their help in improving things. You may be surprised at some of the great ideas your teams can create. And when they create these ideas together, they build a stronger, more loyal, and more successful team.

Empowering your employees with some decision-making authority will instill a sense of ownership and benefit the company greatly.

I have known many executives that would never even think about asking an employee about ideas on how to improve the company. It was a blow to their ego when a person came up with an idea that they did not create. I've also seen people who think that there's no way an employee who has been in their industry for only six months could have any valuable insights. They forget that a new person or outsider can see things and will ask questions that would not even occur to the veteran.

*"Foolish is the teacher who believes he (or she)
can not be taught by the student."*

People miss great opportunities to learn things every day because they think they have nothing to learn from less experienced people. If you open your mind, you will be surprised at how many great new revenue-increasing ideas you can learn from unexpected sources. And remember, the more great ideas your company has, the more successful it will be!

The Blame Game

Why do so many people enjoy making other people feel bad about themselves by *blaming* them for their mistakes? Maybe it helps them to feel better about their own shortcomings.

I believe everyone should be held accountable for their actions, 100 percent of the time. But blaming people for their mistakes only makes them feel bad about themselves. It does nothing to motivate them to do better next time.

When an employee makes a mistake—and I've seen some costly ones—pull him aside and find out what happened. Ask questions and find out how to correct the situation now and prevent it from happening again.

I believe in every mistake there's an opportunity—either an opportunity to learn something or an opportunity to make money. If you're lucky, you'll find both!

If you've ever owned a dog, you probably realize there are two ways you can housebreak him. You can swat his nose with a newspaper when he wets in the house, or you can give him a treat and encourage him when he wets outside. Both actions will usually get you the desired outcome, but which one will allow you to maintain a relationship of trust?

People respond similarly. You can reprimand them when they make mistakes or reward them when they do well. But more than trust is at stake here. If you reprimand too severely, they also won't want to work any harder for you, resulting in lost revenue!

***Let's eliminate blame altogether and
focus on accountability.***

You will demonstrate to your employees that you believe in them and that it's okay to make a mistake now and then as long as they learn from it, improve their skills, and make the company stronger. You will see a great improvement in morale once you've made this switch from blame to accountability.

Motivate, Don't Intimidate

There are two definitive ways to motivate people. You can scare them or you can inspire them! I've seen both styles get immediate results, but one will definitely have better long-term results.

Intimidating people has an immediate impact on their behavior. They will do what you want instantly. You will probably be very happy with the results for a while. But in a short time, the resentment in that employee will have built up and the effectiveness of your tactics will have dropped significantly!

Inspiring employees can be difficult at first, but it will definitely have a higher return in the long run. When you need your employees to do something that is best for the company (but not necessarily fun for them), show them your perspective. Let them see how performing their duty benefits everyone.

Most employees will be able to see the situation from your perspective, and they will want to perform their task with enthusiasm. People appreciate being informed, being a part of the process. Too many companies treat their employees like the proverbial mushroom: feed them manure and keep them in the dark. Why not be the inspiring leader who respects your employees enough to let them in on the big picture?

As I mentioned before in the dog-training analogy, praise positive actions and allow people to learn from their mistakes. I remember reading about an employee in a large corporation who made a three-million-dollar mistake. He knew he had really messed up and feared for his job. The CEO called him into his office to discuss the incident, and the employee said, "I suppose you want my resignation."

The CEO said, "Resignation? I've just invested three million dollars in you. You can't quit now!"

That's the type of leadership that inspires people. Do your best to inspire and you will find the allegiance from your employees grow stronger every day!

Personalized Leadership

Having had dozens of managers over the years, I've seen many different styles of leadership. But the one common thread is they all expected everyone on the team to be motivated and inspired by the same things—almost like a *one-size-fits-all* approach.

Every individual on every team is going to have his strengths and weaknesses. It is foolish to think that everyone responds to the same leadership style. Yet so many leaders still use this *"one-size"* approach. I'll use a baseball analogy here to demonstrate my point.

As a manager of a baseball team, you probably wouldn't ask your slowest runner to steal second every time he got on base. On the flip side, you probably wouldn't ask your smallest player to try to hit a home run every time he stepped up to the plate.

The same is true for business: every single one of your customers is unique. I'm sure you don't use the same approach with all of them to meet their needs.

There's no difference with your employees; each one has his God-given gifts as well as areas that need improvement. Instead of using a cookie-cutter approach to leading, why not take each employee and lead, manage, and inspire him individually, based on his personalities and talents?

One of my favorite examples of personalized leadership is from Mike Krzyzewski, Hall of Fame coach of the Duke University basketball program since 1981. He admits that every year he coaches each team differently than the previous one.

Why does he do it? Because every individual is unique. And since every team is made up of many individuals, every team will also be unique.

At the time of this writing, Coach K's winning percentage with Duke was around .781. Therefore, I'm going to assume that this style of leadership can be very successful!

Look within your organization and find areas where you can personalize your leadership style. This will not only be another great way to demonstrate to your employees that you respect them, but think of how much more inspired they will be to work harder for you when they realize you've recognized their individual talents!

Acknowledgment and Awards

I don't care if you've got an arrogant egomaniac or a docile mute for an employee—everyone loves praise and acknowledgment! That's so important it deserves to be repeated.

Everyone loves praise and acknowledgment.

Praise and acknowledgment lets your employees know that they are important members of your business team! The only limit to how many ways you can demonstrate this is your imagination. Here are some of my favorites.

An employee's anniversary date is a key opportunity for acknowledgment. Think of it like a wedding anniversary. In some ways, an employee/owner relationship is very similar to a husband/wife relationship. God knows most of us spend more time at our jobs than with our significant others.

When the anniversary day arrives, send a thank-you card to your employee, signed by you personally. Thank her for being a loyal, honest, hard-working employee and for giving so many years of dedicated service. If given the chance, she may even tell you that she appreciates the opportunity that you've given her to work for your organization.

I have used this same approach with my clients to acknowledge them on the anniversary date that they first became my client. This has been a very effective way of building customer loyalty. I almost always get great feedback from them. Just as you can differentiate yourself from the competition with your customers, you can do it with your employees.

When a milestone anniversary arrives, do something bigger—a special gift, like a watch for the men or jewelry for the women or a paid trip, such as a cruise! This type of acknowledgment sets a great tone with your less tenured employees and gives them something to strive for.

As company leader, you will likely have many things going on during any given day or week. So, if you are too busy to remember everyone's anniversary date, then assign someone who isn't as busy as you to help you remember. Or you can even create a database in software such as ACT! or Outlook containing all of your employees' information and using automatic reminders.

I am going to say the exact same things about birthdays. Why do most people enjoy celebrating their own birthdays? Because it is their special day. Just because you are in a work environment doesn't mean those eight or nine hours aren't just as meaningful. Birthdays call for even more acknowledgment! The birthday cake, the card signed by everyone in the department (including you)—all of those things *need* to be there. They will build a bond between you, the executive, and the employee that will be hard to find at most other companies. They will help to create an even stronger sense of loyalty.

Many people like to take the day off on their birthday (and there's nothing wrong with that), but that's usually because they'd rather spend it with people who care about them than people who don't. If you show them you do care by providing this type of recognition, they'll actually want to come into work on their birthday!

Another phenomenal motivator is the Employee of the Month Award. Knowing that there's that extra little bit of recognition out there if you try just a little bit harder is what makes people *want* to work harder. Working harder doesn't necessarily mean working longer hours, but it does mean more being more productive.

As a salesperson, one of the greatest benefits my products and services always touted was increased productivity. Isn't that every executive's dream, getting more out of what you already have? Getting the most out of everyone on the team should be every company's number-one priority.

You can take it one step further and present the Employee of the Year Award at your annual holiday banquet or party. Think of how motivating it is knowing there's a prestigious award awaiting some hard worker(s) at the end of the year!

I challenge you to stretch your imagination on this one. See how many ways you can find to acknowledge and award your employees!

Team Building

The term "team building" may be a little dated, but it is still a very important concept. You can have a team of twenty-five superstars and still not be developing your company's true potential. Why? Because everyone's not striving for the same goal. If that's the case you will all be going in different directions and never reach your objectives.

Of all the ways to improve a company's morale, I believe this is the most difficult. After all, how do you get everyone on a team to like each other (or at least get along) and to want to help each other win? Everyone has different backgrounds and life experiences, with varying points of view and motivators.

Truly great team builders are rare. One of my favorites is John Wooden, the legendary basketball coach for the UCLA Bruins. He definitely knew what it took to make a great team. He led his college basketball program to ten national championships in twelve years! Incredible! Mr. Wooden once said, "Team spirit is thinking of others. It means losing oneself in the group for the good of the group. It means being not just willing but eager to sacrifice personal interest or glory for the welfare of all."[2]

Those are some amazing and inspiring words, but how do you get everyone on your team to feel that way? It is tricky but far from impossible. There are several ways to accomplish this in today's business market. Let's look at a few.

Monthly team (or company) outings like sporting events or dinners (at a decent restaurant) can begin to foster a bigger sense of team or family. Just by being around co-workers in a non-working environment, we can get to know them as people. The better we know someone, the greater the chance that we will be able to relate to that person. Once we feel connected to that person, we will be much more likely to offer that person help the next time she needs it.

Mentoring programs for new employees can also foster a sense of team. I've been involved in a few of these programs (on both sides), and they've always helped to create a much stronger team at a much faster rate.

These programs aren't just for the new hires' benefit. The mentor also gains a lot, such as a more developed sense of leadership and experience for possible future management opportunities.

17

There are also many companies that specialize in team building seminars and retreat-like outings. I've experienced a few of these events myself, and I can say that my team came back stronger after each one. They were well worth every penny!

Having a tightly knit team is much better than having a group of selfish individualistic superstars. Building as strong a team as you can is another very important way to ensure your organization's success.

Over-Delivering

As I mentioned earlier, my success as a salesperson can be largely attributed to one thing: my ability to develop long-term customers. My central principle has been over-delivering. People love to be pleasantly surprised.

Give people more than they are used to or expect.

So many sales people out there give the bare minimum. Too often, I'd meet a potential new client and give him more than he was used to getting and gain a loyal client for life. I didn't do anything extraordinary except give him better service than he had been getting.

Why not treat your employees the same way? They are your greatest assets, aren't they?

The most obvious way to over-deliver with your employees is to overpay them. If you have a position at your company that pays $42,000 a year (and your Web savvy employees will definitely know what their job is worth), why not pay them $47,000 a year? Sure, it's a little more out of pocket now, but you already know it will cost you $63,000 (150 percent of their salary, remember?) to replace them when they jump ship for a better offer in the next twelve to eighteen months.

You can also over-deliver in the area of time off—vacation days and paid holidays. So many times, I've seen companies give the bare minimum of both of these. I can guarantee that the employees in those companies don't feel very treasured. So why do employers make such a big deal out of giving away too much vacation time? Probably because they're afraid that too much time off will result in lost revenue. Is that really the case, or is that just fear?

Let's look at this from a different angle for a second. Why not give your newest employees two weeks vacation time for their first year of employment and then add an additional week for the next two years? Yes, your company will miss them while they are relaxing in the sun, but remember:

A happy employee is a productive employee!

A burned-out employee is just the opposite. Worse, he could still be semi-productive but be bringing the rest of the team down because of his bad attitude, caused by burnout! A weary employee is also prone to making costly mistakes.

Be generous with vacation time. Four weeks of vacation after three years of service will not have a big bottom-line impact, but it will have a positive impact on your employees and eventually on your revenue! Your employees will not only enjoy their time off, but they will be better workers because of it.

There's an unspoken philosophy in America that too much vacation time is bad. Why is that? In Japan's largest corporations, they probably work harder than anywhere else in the world, yet they take an average of twenty-five vacation days every year, compared to ten days in the U.S.[3] They see the value in refreshing one's mind, body, and soul. Why not learn from them and make your employees happier by offering more vacations! If you're not convinced about Japan's success, just look at their automobile sales over the past twenty years!

Let's talk about a similar subject: holidays. If you're not giving your employees all (or at least most) of the "B" holidays off, I ask you, "Why not?" Imagine how they must feel when their friends and family members ask them what they are doing on Presidents' Day or Columbus Day—and they say they have to work. Talk about feeling unappreciated. That's like being the last kid picked for dodge ball. It's a couple of extra days off. Just give them to your employees! They will love you for it!

Let's look at the opposite scenario. What if the next time they had that conversation with their peers, they got to say, "I'll be going snowboarding with my family for Presidents' Day. Isn't my company great?" How hard do you think that employee is going to want to work when he gets back?

Holiday bonuses are also an extremely powerful way to develop a loyal employee relationship. At a time when families usually need money the most, nothing says "Happy Holidays" to your employees like a Christmas bonus!

In the late 1990s, I remember one extremely successful company in California that paid its employees their salaries as Christmas bonuses. For example, if an employee made $50,000 a year, his bonus was $50,000! Amazing, huh? It's no wonder that this company was voted one of the best to work for in the nation that year! Imagine how busy their HR department was the following six months dealing with all of those new applications! If you were the CEO or owner, could there have been a bigger affirmation or ego boost? Besides, with a greater pool of applicants, you can afford to be more selective when adding your next team member and make your company even stronger.

The bonus doesn't have to be an absurd amount of money (although that doesn't hurt), but it should be enough so that your employees really believe you care. If someone makes $50,000 a year, a $50 bonus really isn't going to show that you care and value that person's services. Although $50 is better than nothing, one-tenth of 1 percent really doesn't say that you value that employee very much.

I believe you have to start in the 0.5 to 1.0 percent range, at a minimum, to make an impact with a Christmas bonus. Any amount above that is just gravy. Now, I know some people will read this and think that their business is too tight right now and that they can't afford it. Maybe they can't, but can they afford to lose any more valuable employees in today's tight market? Think of it as a long-term investment—an employee retention plan.

You should take every possible opportunity to let your employees know how much you value their services and them as people! Remember, if you don't, some other company will. Or even worse, they could start their own companies and become your direct competition!

The Dreaded Monday

Let's talk about something most executives probably don't want to hear. Are you aware of how many of your employees, right now, dread Monday mornings at your company? I've had several associates and friends in the past tell me that this dreadful feeling begins as early as Sunday afternoon.

They didn't like their jobs so much that this feeling would creep into their personal time on the weekends. I'm willing to bet their dread is not as much about their job as it is the people that they work for. I've had some crummy jobs in the past, but some were still fun because of the people I was lucky enough to work with and for.

The opposite has also been true. I've had great jobs with terrible management and disgruntled employees. I, too, detested Mondays.

Knowing that so many of your employees probably feel this way, why not try an unconventional approach to Mondays?

Why not make Monday mornings so much fun that your employees will actually look forward to them? Every Monday morning, conduct a company-wide meeting that isn't just about business (or involves no business at all) but is about having fun. You could review each other's weekends or play some type of mind-stimulating game to get the week started.

Designate different people every week to bring the refreshments and make a breakfast out of it. Spend the first hour of your workweek just having fun as a team and relating to each other as people. Then, after everyone has relaxed and woken up, they will start their week with a smile!

Yes, this is definitely "out of the box" thinking, but you'll need lots of it to break your employees' "dreaded Mondays" mentality.

Family First

It seems obvious that employees want to put their families first. However, this is not genuinely encouraged enough in the workplace. Even if someone wants to put his family above all else, this usually won't happen unless the employee has the full support of his employer.

There is so much focus on "getting the most out of" every employee that our families too often get put aside. What most employers usually fail to realize is what I've mentioned a few times already: a happy employee is a productive employee! Wouldn't you rather see five or six truly productive hours out of someone than eight or nine half-hearted hours of just being there and going through the motions? I know I would!

If one of your employees' child has a soccer game that starts at four o'clock on a Tuesday afternoon, then he should be highly *encouraged* to leave early to get to experience that with him. If his child is starting his first day of kindergarten at 8:30 on Monday, then he should be showing up to work a little late so he can be there for that vitally important memory.

I know a lot of employees that already do this but then, too often, have to lie about their whereabouts, saying they were at the doctor or dentist, because their employer does not fully approve of putting families first. That, to me, is very sad.

It all starts at the top. If you encourage your employees to put their families first, they will! And I believe that if you support them in these actions, they will be much more likely to show up early the next day, voluntarily, to make up for any missed time.

I'll even go one step further. Instead of merely encouraging your employees to make family their priority, why not make it mandatory? That takes all of the guesswork out of where you as the leader stand on this.

Let's remember this important piece of information:

Life is short. We are all here for a finite amount of time, so why not make the most out of every minute of every day, week, month, and year?

And make the most out of the business days, too!

Encouraging employees to put their families first is one more way to show them that you truly have their best interests at heart. And you will be much more likely to develop a loyal partnership with them.

Remember, a loyal employee is vital to the success of your company!

Respect and Caring

As a successful sales person, I realized something else very early on in my career:

Customers will buy more from you if they believe you genuinely have their best interests at heart.

They can smell a shark a mile away, someone who is just out for the quick kill.

The same goes for the executive/employee relationship. If an employee feels as if management genuinely has her best interests at heart, she will be many times more likely to *want* to work hard for the company.

There are so many ways to demonstrate to an employee that you do care for and respect her. One way is to

Keep your promises.

When you commit to doing something for them, you must do it in the time-frame that you have promised. For example, if you've promised an employee an annual review, you have to have that review on their anniversary date. If not on that day, then you must at least have a day scheduled for this meeting. Who's kidding whom? Employees know why they have reviews in the first place. A review has two purposes: to provide feedback on an employee's performance and to figure out how much of a raise one has earned (if any).

If you delay a review, you are delaying potential income. That does not show respect or caring for an employee. In fact, it displays exactly the opposite! Keeping your promises in a timely manner is crucial to making people feel important.

Another great way to demonstrate respect is to

Treat every employee equally.

It may sound simple and obvious, but you'd be surprised how few leaders actually do this. It's been said that you can tell a lot about a person by the way one treats servers in a restaurant. People notice how you treat the people at every level in your organization. Don't give preferential treatment to the tenured employee over the new hire (or vice versa). Treat your warehouse assistant just as you would your top executive. Your employees will respect you even more for that and give you more effort in their daily activities.

People love working harder for people they respect.

I realize that everyone has different God-given levels of caring, and that's okay. Even if you consider yourself as warm as an ice cube, you can still let your employees know, through your actions, that you really do care. It doesn't matter if you may not genuinely feel this way about your employees and there's a little acting involved; they will still notice and appreciate your efforts.

Although most people may never admit it (especially not to you), everyone wants to be *respected* and *cared about*. Go ahead, give them what they want, and see what kind of positive change this has on your business—and their lives!

Wrapping It Up

There is one other skill I was able to hone during my sales career—I learned how to be a great listener. Becoming a great listener enabled me to understand what my clients wanted from me. This knowledge allowed me to deliver (and over-deliver) on what they needed.

But the funny thing is, my listening didn't stop with my customers; I also learned how to listen to my coworkers. I listened to what they liked and didn't like about working for our company. I listened to the joys as well as the pains they felt working in corporate America. Over the past decade, I came to understand there is a large void in many companies just waiting to be filled. And as I learned many years ago, a problem is just an opportunity waiting to happen!

The result of that understanding is this book—a combination of my own experiences with those of everyone else I've ever worked with. Without them, this book would not be possible.

I decided to write this book for executives from an employee's perspective so that they can make their companies better places for employees to work, increasing their own success in the process. The happier employees are, the harder they will work. The harder they work, the more likely your company is to be successful. Also, the happier they are, the more likely they are to continue to be your employees. And we all know what long-term employees will do for your profits, right?

Here are the key points to help your business become the best one in the world to work for:

Remember how much it costs you to lose a good employee.

Build a sense of ownership with your employees—daily!

Don't blame them, but do hold them accountable.

Inspire greatness within your organization!

Acknowledge successes and loyalty often.

Build the best team you possibly can.

Give your employees much more than they'd ever expect.

Turn Monday into the best day of the week!

Encourage family first within your organization.

Respect and care for your employees.

Right now, I'd like you to ask yourself a couple of questions:

- Is my company as successful as it could be right now?

- Am I doing everything I can to motivate and encourage my employees to be their best?

If you answered no to either of these questions, I encourage you to take my challenge and implement some or all of the ideas presented in this book.

I'd like to add one more thing before I let you go: not only am I writing this book for you, the executive or owner of a company, but I'm also writing it for myself. I, too, will have my own company in the future, and this book will be as much a reminder for me of how to treat my employees as much as it is a guide to help you today!

And it's not just a reminder of how to treat employees; it's a reminder of how to treat *people* properly—with kindness, respect, courtesy, care, and love.

It can be very easy to forget these simple things when we get caught up in the challenges of our everyday lives. I wish every single one of you good luck and much success!

God Bless,
Mark P. Byrne

It's what you learn after you know it all that counts.

—John Wooden

Thank You

I would like to thank Patty Anfinson, Michael Byrne, Mary Lunetto, Geoffrey Stoddart, Richard Anfinson, Barbara Byrne, Gino Lunetto, Sandy Koditek, Keri Anfinson, Rachel Zebro, Kenneth Reilly, Juanita (Babe) Reilly, Anna (Annie) Mealman, Charles Acton, Daniel Acton, Matthew Acton, Elizabeth Acton, Amy Acton, my fifth grade teacher Mrs. Whitton, Tom Ford, Eric Peterson, Kathy Formica, Greg Foy, Julia Chacon, John Wood, Scott Zahn, Erika Garcia, Tammy Waldeck, Tamsen Arabi, Craig Repp, Sydney Anna Byrne, Dawn Byrne, and of course God for guiding me through this long and wonderful journey. You've all had a tremendous impact on my life, and I thank you.

Mark Byrne

I would like to thank God and many people around me for their grace and encouragement. My wife, Mary, and my daughters, Anna and Grace, have borne my foibles and my never-ending string of dreams and projects. I thank them for giving me such grace and space. Numerous friends at Trabuco Presbyterian Church, at Rancho Speechmasters, and in my work environment richly deserve my deepest thanks.

Craig A. Repp

Bibliography

1. Bliss, William. *http://www.blissassociates.com/html/articles/employee_ turnover01.html*

2. Wooden, John R. *Wooden: A Lifetime of Observations and Reflections On and Off the Court.* New York: McGraw-Hill, 1997.

3. Wikipedia. *http://en.wikipedia.org/wiki/Vacation*

About the Authors

Mark Byrne

Mark was born is Los Angeles, CA, in 1966. His family moved to Orange County, CA, when he was seven years old. He spent his childhood days playing baseball and swimming competitively. When he was twelve years old, his little league baseball team won the city championship, and from that day on he knew the value of true teamwork.

After many years of successes and failures, he also realized that God makes no mistakes and there are no coincidences. In fact, it's no coincidence that you're reading his book right now.

He has an amazing wife and one precious daughter, and they are currently living in Orange County, CA.

Craig A. Repp

Craig was raised an "Army brat," living in eight states and going to nine schools by the time he left home for college. He's added five states and three schools since then. This kind of life helped him develop his communications skills and ensured that he has never met a stranger.

He is the most fortunate of men, sharing life with his wife of twenty-five years and his two daughters. His career has centered on service, college ministry, customer support, sales support, and training.

Contact

For more information about this book and it's authors, please go to:

www.whatyouremployeeswant.com

978-0-595-42045-2
0-595-42045-1